T0011215

LIFE IN SPACE

by Catherine C. Finan

BEARPORT
PUBLISHING

Minneapolis, Minnesota

Credits:

Cover, Paopano/Shutterstock, Roblan/Shutterstock, PotaeRin/Shutterstock, Kamal Hasan Bulbul/Shutterstock, NASA Image Collection/Alamy, New Africa/Shutterstock, Klever_ok/Shutterstock; Title Page, 4 top, 5 top, 5 bottom, 6, 7 top right, 7 bottom, 9 top, 9 bottom, 10 top, 11 top, 11 bottom, 12 top, 12 bottom, 13 top, 13 middle, 14 top, 14 bottom, 15 top, 16 top left, 17 top left, 17 top, 17 bottom, 18 top, 19 top, 20 top, 21 top, 21 top right, 21 bottom, 21 bottom left, 25 top, 28 top left, 28 bottom left, NASA/Public Domain; 4 bottom, AleksandrMorrisovich/Shutterstock; 5 top right, Olena Yakobchuk/Shutterstock; 5 bottom left, Kuznetsov Dmitriy/Shutterstock; 5 bottom right, Halfpoint/Shutterstock; 6 bottom left, Laika ac/Creative Commons; 6 bottom middle, Armael/Creative Commons; 6 bottom right, 19 bottom right, LightField Studios/Shutterstock; 7 top left, Mil.ru/Creative Commons; 7 middle, SDASM Archives/Public Domain; 7 bottom left, Robert L. Knudsen/U.S. National Archives and Records Administration/Public Domain; 8 top, NASA/Digitally enhanced by rawpixel/Creative Commons; 8 bottom left, 9 bottom right, 13 bottom right, 27 top right, Roman Samborskyi/Shutterstock; 10 bottom, NASA (via YouTube as ReelNASA)/Public Domain; 11 top left, 11 bottom right, LightField Studios/Shutterstock; 11 bottom left, Nanette Dreyer/Shutterstock; 13 bottom, Photographee.eu/Shutterstock; 15 bottom, NASA/Nick Hague/Public Domain; 16 top, NASA/Jack Fischer/Public Domain; 16 top right, Prostock-studio/Shutterstock; 16 bottom, NASA/Joel Kowsky/Public Domain; 17 top left, Jeka/Shutterstock; 18 bottom, WAYHOME studio/Shutterstock; 19 bottom left, 19 bottom middle, Robert Markowitz/NASA/Public Domain; 20 bottom, NASA/Bill Ingalls/Public Domain; 22, sripfoto/Shutterstock; 22 top, NASA/Goddard/Francis Reddy/Public Domain; 22 bottom left, Anna Om/Shutterstock; 22 bottom right, Paul Michael Hughes/Shutterstock; 23 top, Triff/Shutterstock; 23 middle, NASA/JPL-Caltech/Public Domain; 23 bottom, collage/Joshua Avramson; 23 bottom right, NOAA Okeanos Explorer Program, Galapagos Rift Expedition 2011/Public Domain, richcarey/iStock, alxpin/iStock; 24–25, 25 bottom right, 27 bottom left, Gorodenkoff/Shutterstock; 24 top, Vadim Sadovski/Shutterstock; 24 left, Daderot/Creative Commons; 25 middle, JeanLucMargot/Creative Commons; 26 top, JPL/NASA/Public Domain; 26 middle, AleksandrMorrisovich/Shutterstock.com; 26 bottom left, Vadim Sadovski/Shutterstock; 27, Dotted Yeti/Shutterstock; 27 top, Jurik Peter/Shutterstock; 27 top left, Max Topchii/Shutterstock; 27 bottom middle, Sergey Nivens/Shutterstock; 28 top right, Imageman/Shutterstock; 28 bottom middle, Kozak Sergii/Shutterstock; 28 bottom right, PHILIPIMAGE/Shutterstock, Jacob Kearns/Shutterstock; 28–29, Austen Photography

President: Jen Jenson
Director of Product Development: Spencer Brinker
Senior Editor: Allison Juda
Associate Editor: Charly Haley
Designer: Elena Klinkner

Developed and produced for Bearport Publishing by BlueAppleWorks Inc.
Managing Editor for BlueAppleWorks: Melissa McClellan
Art Director: T.J. Choleva
Photo Research: Jane Reid

Library of Congress Cataloging-in-Publication Data

Names: Finan, Catherine C., 1972- author.
Title: Life in space / by Catherine C. Finan.
Description: Minneapolis, Minnesota : Bearport Publishing, [2022] | Series: X-treme facts : space | Includes bibliographical references and index.
Identifiers: LCCN 2021039156 (print) | LCCN 2021039157 (ebook) | ISBN 9781636915081 (library binding) | ISBN 9781636915159 (paperback) | ISBN 9781636915227 (ebook)
Subjects: LCSH: International Space Station--Juvenile literature. | Space stations--Juvenile literature. | Life support systems (Space environment)--Juvenile literature.
Classification: LCC TL797.15 .F565 2022 (print) | LCC TL797.15 (ebook) | DDC 629.44/2--dc23
LC record available at https://lccn.loc.gov/2021039156
LC ebook record available at https://lccn.loc.gov/2021039157

For more information, write to Bearport Publishing, 5357 Penn Avenue South, Minneapolis, MN 55419. Printed in the United States of America.

Contents

Space: The Final Frontier 4

That's Out of This World! 6

A Home in Space 8

Life on a Space Station 10

Sweet Dreams 12

Time to Eat! 14

Where's the Toilet? 16

The Twin Experiment 18

Spectacular Spacewalks 20

Is Anybody Out There? 22

A Pit Stop on the Moon 24

Would You Move to Mars? 26

Jet Pack 28

Glossary 30

Read More 31

Learn More Online 31

Index 32

About the Author 32

Space: The Final Frontier

Throughout history, people have looked up at the night sky and wondered what mysteries were among the twinkling stars. Many even dreamed of going to space someday. This inspired inventions that have allowed us to study and explore what lies beyond Earth. People have traveled to space to do scientific **research** and to live in space stations **orbiting** Earth. Can you imagine a life in space?

One goal of space travel is to unite different nations as they explore space. People from all around the world are a part of it.

PEACE ON EARTH AND BEYOND!

It's not all about peace, though. Some countries have gone to space for **military** reasons, including spying on other countries from high above Earth.

I SPY WITH MY LITTLE EYE . . .

People have to wear the right gear to travel in space safely. Spacesuits protect their bodies from extreme conditions.

IF YOU'RE GOING TO SPACE, YOU GOTTA LOOK SHARP. . .

. . . AND STAY SAFE!

Astronauts help scientists research ways that people could live in space for long periods of time.

Because **climate change** is harming Earth, **some people believe we may need to live in space in the future.**

HEY, THAT LOOKS FUN!

YEAH! WITH OUR RESEARCH, YOU COULD FLOAT AROUND IN SPACE SOMEDAY, TOO!

That's Out of This World!

A lot had to happen before the first people could actually travel to space. In 1926, the first rocket powered by liquid **fuel** shot into the sky. It was a good first step, even if it flew only 41 feet (12.5 m) high. Later rockets traveled farther, beyond Earth's **atmosphere**. Eventually, animals made the trip to space. And finally, in 1961, the first person went to space. What a ride!

In 1960, dogs Belka and Strelka became the first living creatures to survive an orbit around Earth.

DON'T WORRY! ONCE I BECOME AN ASTRONAUT, I'LL TAKE YOU TO SPACE, TOO.

IT'S OUR MISSION . . .

. . . TO GO WHERE NO DOG HAS GONE BEFORE!

On April 12, 1961, Yuri Gagarin from the **Soviet Union** became the first person to travel to space and orbit Earth. **His flight lasted almost two hours.**

I'M RIGHT BEHIND YOU, YURI!

WELL, SOMEBODY HAD TO GO FIRST . . .

On May 5, 1961, Alan Shepard became the first American astronaut in space.

The Soviet Union's Valentina Tereshkova became **the first woman in space in 1963.**

On May 25, 1961, President John F. Kennedy said the United States would put a man on the moon by the end of the 1960s.

On July 20, 1969, American astronauts Neil Armstrong and Edwin "Buzz" Aldrin became the first people to walk on the moon.

GOOD JOB, GUYS! YOU DID IT!

THANKS, PRESIDENT KENNEDY!

A Home in Space

Traveling to space is one thing, but what about living there? The Soviet Union **launched** the first space station, Salyut, in 1971. A crew lived there for 24 days before returning to Earth. Next, in 1973, came the American station Skylab, where a crew stayed for 84 days. Then, the Soviet station Mir was launched in 1986. It housed different crews from 1987 to 2000. Whether it's for a few weeks or many months, living in space is a very different experience than being home on Earth!

Mir was the first space station put together entirely in space. It was made from parts that were all launched separately.

WOW, IT'S LIKE A GIANT LEGO SET IN SPACE!

Crews living on Salyut, Skylab, and Mir **were studied to learn about the effects of space on the human body.**

Mir had room for three crewmembers. Soviet astronaut Valeri Polyakov lived there for a record-setting 437.7 days in a row.

THERE'S NOT MUCH ROOM, BUT THE VIEW IS PRETTY GREAT.

Everyone on a space station lives in low **gravity**. They move around **by floating through the air!**

I NEED SOME SPACE! THIS TABLE IS TOO CROWDED.

WHY IS HE FLOATING AWAY FROM US?

I WOULD MAKE A GOOD ASTRONAUT!

On Earth, gravity pulls more blood to your feet. But the low gravity in space makes blood spread evenly up and down, **so your face puffs up and your legs get thinner.**

Life on a Space Station

Today, the International Space Station (ISS) is the only place where people are living in space. It usually has a crew of up to six people from different countries living and working together. In their free time, they do many of the same things we do—eat meals, exercise, watch movies, play music, read, and email family and friends. Are you up for some space fun?

Low gravity makes people lose muscle. To stay healthy, ISS crewmembers exercise two hours a day.

ARE MY TWO HOURS UP YET?

Each day, ISS crewmembers spend about nine and a half hours working and exercising.

What can you do for fun in space? Try low-gravity sports, such as floating soccer!

Sometimes, the ISS crew has fun by watching movies on a 65-inch (165 cm) screen.

Life in space still includes a morning routine. On the ISS, people brush their teeth, bathe with wet towels, and wash their hair with waterless shampoo.

Although they're in space, astronauts still work with people on Earth. **Satellites** allow them to communicate almost instantly.

People in space talk with family and friends on Earth through email and video chat.

Sweet Dreams

After a busy day, it's time for bed. But sleeping in space is a little trickier than it is down on Earth. For folks on the ISS, orbiting Earth at 17,500 miles per hour (28,100 kph) is part of the challenge. They also have to sleep through a new sunrise every 90 minutes. And there's the low gravity—how do you sleep if you're floating around? Getting some shut-eye in space isn't easy!

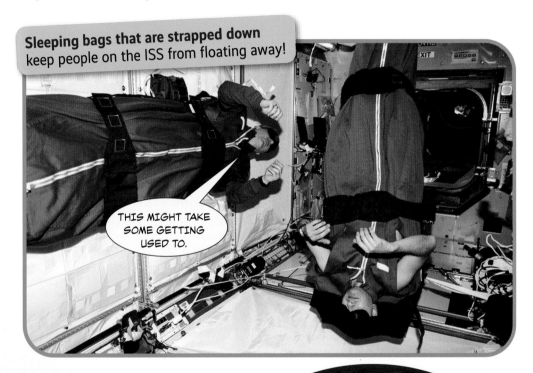

Sleeping bags that are strapped down keep people on the ISS from floating away!

THIS MIGHT TAKE SOME GETTING USED TO.

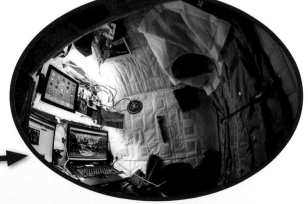

Another problem? Making sure you keep breathing **oxygen** while you sleep. Sleeping cabins on the ISS have air vents for this.

People need less sleep in space than on Earth, probably because our muscles don't work as hard in low gravity.

DON'T FORGET YOUR EARPLUGS!

WHAT? I CAN'T HEAR YOU OVER ALL THIS NOISE!

All of the equipment on the ISS can be loud. Crewmembers sleep with earplugs to block out the noise.

After returning to Earth, sleeping may still feel a bit different. **Some astronauts say they feel like they're floating above their mattress!**

MOM! DAD IS FLOATING AGAIN!

WELL, THIS IS A BIT ODD . . .

Time to Eat!

While sleeping in space is a challenge, eating in space can get just plain messy! That's why space food is packaged and prepared in ways that keep the mess as small as possible. Some foods, such as fruits, can be eaten in their normal forms. Other foods, such as spaghetti, are dried before they're sent to space. Then, you just need to add water and heat them up! With three meals a day, the menu can be pretty interesting . . .

Space meals need to be strapped down so they won't float away!

THAT'S RIGHT! IF YOU DON'T STRAP IT DOWN, YOU'LL HAVE TO CATCH IT!

Astronauts on the ISS eat from special trays that hold food in place.

There are no refrigerators in space. **All food needs to be packaged so it doesn't go bad at room temperature.**

Luckily, there are a lot of options for space foods, such as chicken, beef, seafood, peanut butter, and vegetables. There are even brownies for dessert!

CATCH YOURSELVES SOME FRUIT, GUYS!

THANKS, LET ME FINISH MY DRINK POUCH FIRST.

HERE, HAVE A BROWNIE!

People in space drink water, coffee, tea, and juices from sealed pouches with straws.

People's senses of smell and taste are weaker in space, so food tastes less flavorful. **That's why astronauts like things spicy!**

Most ISS foods have to be wet or sticky and without crumbs. Floating crumbs can get into equipment, which could be dangerous!

THIS PIZZA IS A LITTLE SOGGY!

DID YOU PUT JALAPENO PEPPERS ON EVERYTHING?

YES, I DID! MOIST AND SPICY, JUST THE WAY WE LIKE IT!

Where's the Toilet?

What comes after drinking and eating in space? Peeing and pooping, of course! As on Earth, once liquids and food make their way through a person's body, it's time for the toilet. But in space, doing your business is a little more complicated. Space bathrooms need handholds and footholds to keep people from floating off the toilet. What else happens when an astronaut has to go?

On the ISS, people pee very carefully into a **funnel**. If any pee leaks out, it could damage equipment!

CAREFUL WITH THE FUNNELS!

IF THIS TOILET BREAKS, WE'RE IN SOME DEEP DOO-DOO!

The ISS toilet **suctions** away whatever falls into it. But if something goes wrong, crewmembers may have floating poop to clean up!

BEING AN ASTRONAUT IS AWESOME. BUT POOPING IN SPACE? NOT SO AWESOME.

Astronaut Peggy Whitson said going to the bathroom was the worst part of living in space.

Space bathrooms have improved a lot since the 1960s, when the first toilets used by **NASA** were just bags taped to astronauts' backsides!

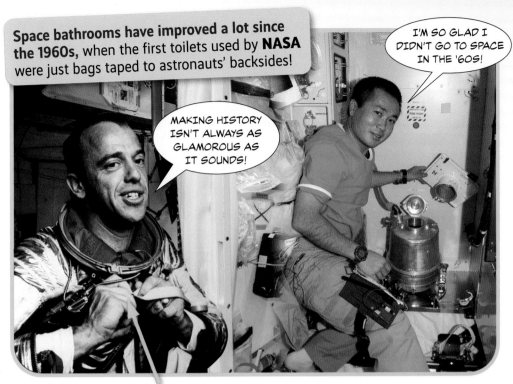

When Alan Shepard went to space in 1961, no one had made a bathroom plan for him. He had to pee in his spacesuit!

If you have to throw up in space, you don't use the toilet. Instead, you vomit into a sturdy barf bag. *Ew!*

The Twin Experiment

Astronauts (and their poop!) are studied by scientists on Earth so we can learn even more about what happens to humans in space. In one incredible experiment, astronaut Scott Kelly lived on the ISS for a year while his identical twin brother Mark stayed on Earth. Scientists compared Mark's body on Earth to Scott's body in space. They did many tests on the twins, and the results were interesting . . .

We all have **bacteria** in our gut. **The kinds found in Scott's poop from space were different from Mark's—and other people's—on Earth.**

SCOTT, WHO KNEW YOUR POOP WAS SO EDUCATIONAL?

DON'T BE JEALOUS, MARK. YOURS HELPED, TOO!

WOW! MAYBE HE HAD ALIENS IN HIS GUT!

After Scott returned to Earth, his gut bacteria went back to normal.

During his time in space, Scott's **arteries** became narrower compared to Mark's on Earth.

ARE YOU GOING TO CHECK MY ARTERIES WITH THAT?

NO, I WANT TO CHECK YOUR EYES. ONE LOOKS A BIT SWOLLEN.

One of Scott's eyeballs swelled a bit in space.
Eye problems are common during long-term trips to space.

After returning to Earth, **Scott's reactions were a bit slower for about six months.**

SCOTT! HELLO! PAY ATTENTION TO ME!

I'M SORRY! I'M JUST A LITTLE SLOW THESE DAYS.

MY BROTHER NEVER PAYS ANY ATTENTION TO ME EITHER. AND HE WASN'T EVEN IN SPACE!

Spectacular Spacewalks

During Scott Kelly's long stay in space, part of his job was to take care of his home away from home. Whenever an astronaut exits a spacecraft in space, it's called a spacewalk. But it's not like walking on Earth—it's more like floating! Spacewalks are done to test and fix equipment. Sometimes, spacewalks are part of experiments to see how space affects different things. Are you ready to take a walk in space? Let's suit up and get out there!

During spacewalks, ropes keep astronauts **attached to their spacecraft.**

THIS IS FUN!

AS COOL AS IT GETS!

WE ARE COOL, AREN'T WE?

It takes 45 minutes to put on a spacesuit for a spacewalk. The full suit includes undergarments that help keep the astronaut cool.

The first person to go on a spacewalk was Russian astronaut **Alexei Leonov** in March 1965. His spacewalk lasted 12 minutes.

GO ON, YOU CAN DO IT!

YEAH, I'M READY!

Today, spacewalks can last between five and eight hours!

Special backpacks with jet thrusters are a must for spacewalks. If you start floating away, a jet pack can help you fly back to the spacecraft.

HEY, THERE'S NOTHING TO IT!

I DON'T THINK I'M READY TO LET GO OF THIS ROPE.

Bruce McCandless was the first person to take a spacewalk without being connected to a spacecraft. He used a jet pack to move around. *Whoa!*

Is Anybody Out There?

So far, much of our space exploration—from dogs in orbit to astronauts on the ISS—has focused on bringing life from Earth into space. But what about other living things that may be in our solar system and beyond? Scientists are searching for other life-forms on our solar system's planets and moons. And the search doesn't end there. Outside of our solar system, there are thousands of other planets. Could some of them be like Earth and support life?

There are trillions of stars in the universe, and scientists think almost every star could have at least one planet orbiting it.

Planets orbiting stars outside of our solar system are called exoplanets.

SHHH! THEY HAVEN'T FOUND ME YET!

HEY, DID I HEAR SOMEBODY OVER THERE?

When scientists search for life on other planets and moons, they look for oxygen and water. We need these things to survive.

C'MON, DON'T HIDE! DO YOU HAVE ANY OXYGEN?

Earth is in our sun's Goldilocks zone. This means it's just the right distance from the sun for the temperature to allow liquid water to exist.

AND LOSE ALL MY WATER? I DON'T THINK SO!

COME A BIT CLOSER, EARTH. DON'T BE SHY!

Earth is the only planet we know of that always has liquid water on its surface.

Scientists believe Jupiter's moon Europa has an ocean beneath its icy surface. Could it be full of life, like Earth's ocean?

HELLO! I'M VISITING FROM EUROPA.

WHAT'S IT LIKE THERE?

Europa's ocean may hold twice as much water as all of Earth's oceans combined.

DO THE HUMANS KNOW ABOUT YOU?

A Pit Stop on the Moon

As scientists search for life beyond Earth, they're also working on sending people back to the moon. And the astronauts wouldn't just be visiting—they'd eventually live there! NASA has plans to set up a base camp where people could live and work. Research on the moon would prepare us for the next step in space exploration . . . humans on Mars!

NASA's plan to send people to the moon and Mars is called the Artemis program. It's named after the Greek goddess of the moon.

YOU NAMED IT AFTER ME? I'M HONORED!

WE ARE HONORED TO BE HERE, ARTEMIS!

The Artemis program plans to send people to the moon by 2024.

The Artemis program's base camp will serve as an example for a possible future camp on Mars.

Some people have suggested building the Artemis base camp near a **crater** at the moon's south **pole.** The crater has ice that might be able to provide water.

Plans for the Artemis base camp include a living area and **rovers** that can travel away from camp to explore.

HERE WE ARE, FINALLY!

IT'S ABOUT TIME!

NASA plans to send the first person of color and the first woman to the moon as part of the first Artemis crew.

Would You Move to Mars?

Not so long ago, living on Mars probably seemed impossible. But today, there are plans to send people to Mars within a few decades! When people finally make the long spaceflight to Mars, they might make a base camp so people could live and work on the Red Planet. What an adventure! Would you want to live on Mars?

As Mars and Earth orbit the sun, the distance between them changes. At their farthest from each other, they're 249 million miles (401 million km) away.

Every two years, Earth and Mars are as close as they can get—about 34 million miles (55 million km) apart. That's when a spacecraft from Earth would be launched.

C'MON GUYS, HURRY UP! I'M AS CLOSE TO YOU AS I CAN GET!

JUST ANOTHER 34 MILLION MILES TO GO . . .

A spaceflight from Earth to Mars and back would probably take almost two years!

Mars is much farther from the sun than Earth is, **so it gets very cold.**

GO GET A BLANKET! YOU'LL BE JUST FINE!

I DON'T THINK WE'RE DRESSED FOR THIS.

Mars has no breathable oxygen. To survive, you'd have to bring oxygen with you everywhere you went.

There's no regular source of water on Mars's surface. Scientists are researching ways to get water for Mars travelers.

NO OXYGEN, NO WATER—WHAT KIND OF VACATION IS THIS?

IF YOU'RE GOING TO COMPLAIN, YOU SHOULD JUST STAY ON EARTH NEXT TIME!

Jet Pack
Craft Project

When you go on a spacewalk, you can't forget your jet pack! If you float a little too far away from your spacecraft, the jet pack will steer you back to safety. Here on Earth, you can make your own jet pack, too!

An astronaut's jet pack has a joystick that can be used to steer.

What You Will Need

- Scissors
- A piece of cardboard 5 inches (12.5 cm) x 7 in. (18 cm)
- Ribbon
- 2 empty plastic bottles
- Aluminum foil
- Masking tape
- Permanent markers

Astronauts usually spacewalk in teams of two so they can help each other stay safe.

Step One

Use scissors to cut a 1/2 in. (1.3 cm) vertical slit near each corner of the cardboard as shown.

Step Two

Cut two pieces of ribbon about the same length as backpack straps. Tie a knot at each end of the ribbon pieces. Then, slide a ribbon end through a slit on the cardboard, and pull it until the knot is against the cardboard. Repeat for each corner of the cardboard.

Step Three

Cover the plastic bottles with aluminum foil. Arrange the bottles under the cardboard piece, and hold them in place with masking tape wrapped around the middle. Make sure the tape doesn't cover the ribbon straps.

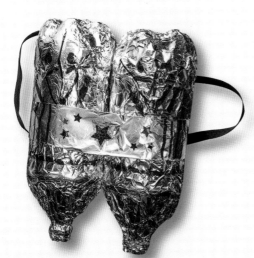

Step Four

Fold a piece of aluminum foil into a strip. Wrap it in front of the tape. Connect the strip with tape at the back. Decorate the jet pack with permanent markers. Blast off!

Glossary

arteries blood vessels that carry blood away from the heart to the rest of the body

atmosphere the gases surrounding a planet

bacteria tiny living things

climate change changes in the usual weather patterns around Earth, including the warming of the air and oceans, due to human activities

fuel something that is burned as a source of energy

funnel a tool shaped like a cone with a narrow tube at the small end

gravity the force that pulls things toward Earth, the sun, or other bodies in space

launched sent into the air with great force

military having to do with war or protecting a country

NASA National Aeronautics and Space Administration, the United States' organization that conducts space travel and research

orbiting moving in a path around another object; the path traveled is called an orbit

oxygen a colorless, odorless gas humans need to live

pole either end of the imaginary line around which a planet or moon turns

research to study something; the information gathered in that study is also called research

rovers vehicles for exploring the surface of a planet or moon

satellites objects in space that orbit larger objects

Soviet Union a country that no longer exists that was made up of several nations in eastern Europe and northern Asia

suctions removes by sucking something away with force

Read More

Finan, Catherine C. *The International Space Station (X-treme Facts: Space).* Minneapolis: Bearport Publishing, 2022.

Lawrence, Ellen. *Surviving in Space (Space-ology).* New York: Bearport Publishing, 2019.

Rechner, Amy. *Astronaut (Torque: Cool Careers).* Minneapolis: Bellwether Media, 2020.

Learn More Online

1. Go to **www.factsurfer.com** or scan the QR code below.

2. Enter **"Life in Space"** into the search box.

3. Click on the cover of this book to see a list of websites.

Index

Aldrin, Edwin "Buzz" 7

Armstrong, Neil 7

Artemis program 24–25

bathrooms 16–17

exoplanets 22

Europa 23

food 14–16

Gagarin, Yuri 7

Goldilocks zone 23

International Space Station (ISS) 10–16, 18, 20

jet packs 21, 28–29

Kelly, Mark 18–19

Kelly, Scott 18–20

Mars 24–27

Mir 8–9

NASA 17, 24–25

Polyakov, Valeri 9

satellites 11

Shepard, Alan 7, 17

Skylab 8

sleep 12–14

Soviet Union 7–8

spacewalks 20–21, 28

Tereshkova, Valentina 7

Whitson, Peggy 16

About the Author

Catherine C. Finan is a writer living in northeastern Pennsylvania. One of her most-prized possessions is a telescope that lets her peer into space.